How to promote a book Winners Circle

STEVEN SCHOOL

Copyright © 2012 Steven School

All rights reserved.

ISBN:1494855631
ISBN-13:9781494855635

DEDICATION

I dedicate this book to my winners circle of highly motivated authors who are networking together to promote each other's work. This is the single most powerful tool that will drive our sales up into the big numbers. Do you have the desire and motivation to join the million sales club?

CONTENTS

1 How to promote a book

ACKNOWLEDGMENTS

I would like to acknowledge the folks at Amazon, Kobo, Barnes and Noble, Youtube, Pinterest, Shelfari, and Face book, for giving us the tools to create, share, and network.

1 GETTING STARTED.

Let us begin this powerful and illuminating book by going over the basics of getting started.

The free self publishing platform, this is the modern tool for creating a published product, such as a printed book, an electronic E book, an audio book cd, an instant video download, or a DVD.

The days of paying thousands of dollars for a traditional publisher to create your masterpiece are quickly becoming obsolete. We now have a wide array of powerful tools right at our fingertips.

One important beginning point to note in sales, is variety. This key concept enables us to reach a much larger audience of potential buyers.

Let me give you an example of my meaning of variety, I offer books in both printed version, as well as electronic version, because there is a market for both. Some people would rather have a traditional printed book, and others go with the modern trend of wireless delivery. Some people actually buy both. Many persons who were interested in my books have purchased the electronic edition first, just to see if they liked the book, and then ordered the printed version. Here I have received two sales for one single book, from one customer. I also like to write books in series, because most people who read one book and enjoy it, will buy the rest of the books in the set, as well as provide word of mouth advertising by telling their friends, or even loaning out books that they are finished reading.

Another aspect of variety is in the price, so far my products range in price from 99 cents to $26.95 and include a myriad of prices in between.

Subject matter, another key concept of both variety, and increasing sales by reaching a much larger audience is subject matter. Herein lies a vital secret of some of today's top selling authors. Some persons take the approach of writing one or two books, and then waiting for results which never come. Many people will spend years creating a single book. To each his own yes, but my way is different. I publish several books per year, and they are on a wide variety of subjects. The more books that I write, the more potential sales that I will get, the more variety of subject matter that I cover, the larger audience that I might appeal to.

My basic starting plan is to produce a minimum of thirteen products per year, if not more, and to offer them in as many of these formats as possible, printed book, electronic book, audio book cd, mp3, DVD, and instant video download, since there is a market for each. I will also include variety in the prices between these items, all products have a minimum price to get them published and distributed, which is where we must start. Several smaller books with small prices usually sell much more often than one single big book with a big price. If the book is three hundred to five hundred pages long and costs thirty dollars or more, I probably will not buy it, although occasionally I will and when I do, I probably will never read all of it. Some persons will get bored in that many pages. This type of book could be broken up into a series or a trilogy and marketed for around ten dollars apiece per printed copy and 2.99 per electronic version, and achieve a higher degree of success. Studies have shown that the price affects the sales, large publishing companies analyze sales data to determine current marketing trends in order to optimize sales, a diligent author can research and find articles containing this information posted online, keep yourself up to date, and up to speed. Here is an interesting fact that I discovered about electronic books, the E books that sold the most in 2013 were priced at 2.99

In the previous year of 2012, the top selling books in electronic format were priced at 99 cents. In both years these two price categories were in the number one and the number two, highest sales positions. What does this tell us?, it tells me that all of my electronic books should be priced either at 99 cents, or at 2.99, not above, not below, and not in between. Choose one of these prices according to which one suits the content of your book, as well as by what your goals are.

I like to create 99 cent electronic books. These are easy and even sometimes fun to create, I believe the amount of sales that I get will be higher since the price is so cheap, also at this price it does not require 300 pages of content. If my commission on a 99 cent E book is usually 35 to 40 cents per sale, then if I can simply just get 100,000 sales per year, that is roughly 40 thousand dollars per year of extra income. Another interesting point regarding my E books is that each and every one of them is promoting my other products, I can include information about my DVD's, printed books, or other products within the pages of this book and by doing that, I am not only getting free publicity for my products but I am also getting paid to promote my other books.

Sales have always been where the big money is at, and in today's world of internet communications the money is in internet sales. This begins with key words that the search engines pick up on to get your product in front of the customer. What is more powerful than a keyword?, a keyword phrase. We really need to be on the first page of search results when our subject matter is queried in order to achieve optimum visibility and product exposure. Research your subject matter, find the most common key word phrases that potential customers might type into the search engine if they are looking for your type of product. How can we take this one step higher?, simple. As you are posting your product for sale at certain places online, you will be asked to enter key words related to your product, here we use key word phrases instead of single words, and we separate these short phrases by commas, also when you are first designing your book, as the idea for your new masterpiece begins to form within your mind, you can use the best key word phrase that you can find as the actual title of your book.

What do the customers want?, I frequently interact with my customers through social media sites as well as direct email. Sometimes they will ask me if I have a specific type of book on a subject that they are interested in, if the answer is no, then I will seriously consider researching the subject and creating the book. All of the questions that my readers ask me, are fuel for creating new books. All it really takes for me, is that a simple idea comes to mind, and then I will create an entire book around it.

At any point during the construction of your book, it is highly advisable to create a video book trailer. Some will do this after their book is already published. Some will do this in the beginning, which will give us a head start, we need to get this train up to speed, it takes time to get the momentum rolling.

I like to create my literary masterpieces at create space. This site is user friendly and very easy to work with. Once I apply the title information and design the cover I can get the create space web address for my product sales page, even though the book is not yet available for sale, I can go into my windows live movie maker program and make a video slideshow presentation for my book. Since my book title is the key word phrase which I feel best suits my work, I will use this as the title of the youtube video.

There are a couple more free options that we have to optimize the appearance of this video in search results. The search engines can see inside of this video because it is a digital product which only exists online. I have already used my best keyword phrase as both the title of the product, and the title of the video, now I will fill in the description section as well as the actual keyword information before the final video upload to youtube. Both of these sections I will fill in with a mixture of key words and key word phrases. When it comes to the actual construction of the video itself, it begins with selecting the title to be displayed at the start of the video, and of course this once again is our main key word phrase, as we create this video we can insert pictures as well as captions, these captions we will use to describe our product, and we will also use them to apply more keywords.

At the end of the video we still have the credits section, this is a good place to display the web address of the sales page for your product. You can adjust the time length for each frame of your video to be displayed, make sure you allow enough time for the potential customers to grab a pen and write down the information. You will need some pictures to fill in your video slide show presentation/book trailer. This is very simple, use the photo of your book cover, use your author photo, and at the end of the movie, create a slide show presentation of your other products. You can also include an about the author section. To do this, I searched online for a black background. I saved this picture to my computer, it is simply a picture of blackness, I can insert this picture into my video, then click insert caption in the movie maker program, and now I can put words onto this frame. This is a very professional book trailer. Upload it to youtube and face book as well as to your web site to get the train rolling and building up steam as you work on writing the actual book.

Once my book is created in printed format, it is now available at create space direct, as well as at amazon. I will now upload my product to kindle so that they can promote and market it as well. Once this is done, I continue on to the nook website, this is Barnes and Nobles electronic book program. Since I already have my book file and cover picture in my computer, I can simply upload this information into the nook program, and they will begin marketing and promoting my book. Now I journey on to the Kobo writing life website and upload my work here. By doing these simple things, suddenly I find my products advertised on web sites that I never even heard of, simply because these platforms are promoting my work, and it did not cost me anything, but it is increasing my sales.

I will create 99 cent E books just to promote my other books, if sales are not as high as I would like, I can easily choose a subject to be the nucleus of my new book, write thirty to fifty pages on this topic, insert advertisements for my other products within the book, usually by simply listing them at the end, and then publish this E book to all of the platforms that I mentioned and they will begin promoting this 99 cent book all over the world which in turn will generate revenue on its own, as well as promote and publicize my other works.

The more we write, the better we get. An author once told me that if you write ten books you will start getting really good at it and this is true. I have noticed that the time it takes me to design and create a book is much faster now than it was when I first started. My skills have improved considerably already, and will only get better. This will be my fourteenth E book.

I also have published more than twenty printed books, and a couple of DVD's in the future I will be expanding to mp3, audio book cd, and instant video download. Today is my birthday, and I have decided that the gift I would like to give myself on this day, is to publish this book, and to effectively promote it.

Once our literary journey has brought us this far, there are social media outlets which we can use to further promote our work.

Let us begin with shelfari, all that we need to do here is to register with the site, and set up our bookshelf, which simply means to import our books electronically using the simple instructions provided on their website. I am also going to include a piece of advice that not only affects your productivity at this site, but also at the other social media outlets as well. The more active that you are on all of the social media platforms, the more people will notice you, the more followers and friends you will get, which means that more people will see and share your work, as well as buy. On some of these sites, you can list your book cover as your photo, as you explore the web, clicking like, share and comment on various things, you are promoting your books. You are also drawing more attention to your book shelf.

The next stop is a website called pinterest, this is somewhat similar to shelfari, fill out your profile here and set up your bookshelf, become active in this community and attract others to your profile. On shelfari there are blogs, you can join in these discussions or create a new one, you are just inviting people to your bookshelf with this powerful tool.

It is very important to build a network of motivated authors who will work together to promote each other's work, this is one of the most powerful tools that we have at our disposal, and we will discuss this in great detail later in this book, formulating a specific plan to drive our sales upward toward the million sales club.

Twitter is a gold mine. Sign up for your twitter account, use a book cover as your profile picture, become active. You can search twitter by keyword to find persons who would be specifically interested in the subject matter of your book, when you find these persons click follow, twitter will send them an email notification that you are now following them, and it will also ask them if they would like to follow you, since you have the common interest in subject matter, many of them will. This method will increase our followers.

What we need to do next with this site, is to become very active tweeting things, the more active we are, the more followers that we attract. If I log into my twitter account and see a tweet that looks interesting, I will re tweet it, this can increase my followers. The bigger my audience becomes, the more sales I get. If I tweet my book, I attract sales, re tweets, and new followers which means more sales. If I tweet your book, you get more sales but I am attracting more followers to my twitter account, the tweet has the potential to be seen by millions of people, they can click follow, re tweet, or go directly to your sales page, of the people who click follow on the tweets and re tweets, they will be following me since I am the one who posted your book. Now when I tweet my own book I am reaching a larger audience and this will help my products to go viral worldwide across the web.

Let me just throw something out there as food for thought. Could I write a five hundred page book and market it for say twenty to thirty dollars per copy, or should I write ten, fifty page books and market them for 9.95 each? What if I created thirty or forty of these and then created two dozen 99 cents E books to generate additional income as well as promote these ten dollar books? What if I even created a series of fifty page printed books and just marketed them at 5.95 apiece? What would optimize my sales and increase my profits, creating a series of shorter books on a wide variety of topics and pricing them anywhere from six to ten dollars apiece, as well as creating a couple dozen 99 cent E books, all products promoting each other, or work on the larger task of writing one full length book or novel per year? The simple and logical answer is that one of these options is less work and can make more money, the other option is more work and might make less money. The goal of business is not to work, it is to make money, and publishing books is a business. It is a good idea to publish one full length book or novel per year, as well as to publish one short story type book per month, giving yourself the best of both worlds.

As I mentioned earlier in this book, the more that you write, the better you become, and this is very true. When I first began writing as a hobby which was a little over a year ago, it might have taken me two months to create a 99 cent E book, I have been writing since around the end of the year 2012, and now I can make a 99 cent E book in one day if I am motivated, which I am. The last book that I published took me two days to create before it was ready to submit to the publisher, this book will be ready for submission today, on my birthday, a one day book which serves a purpose for both of us. I was not born knowing how to promote a book, or to create one. It is a skill that I had to research and learn on my own. These things that I am sharing with you in this book have made money for me, if I go to a job working for an employer, I must fit the required schedule, and complete the required tasks in order to be paid. If I am successful with that I will be paid, I will receive one day of pay for one day of work, I will receive one month of pay for one month of work, if I use my time to create a book, I will do the work one time, at my own pace, as it fits my own schedule, but I will be paid book royalties repeatedly for the rest of my life. Should I work one time and get paid one time?, or should I work one time and get paid a thousand times? I would like to write a lot of books! I am in love with publishing now, it has gone from hobby, to entrepreneurial dream. The more that you promote your book, the more that it will sell, working alone you can cover most of the basics which will bring in profitable sales, but working as a group, we can form a very powerful tool to propel us upward toward the million sales mark, and that is why I am forming what I call my winners circle, a special group of insiders working together, to get the big numbers and to become the next huge publishing success story. If I help you to succeed, I help myself to succeed, Karma, what goes around comes around. On face book, you can create community pages for your books, I have several of these, I post my books here with links directly to my sales pages. The face book community pages that I have constructed are the place where my winners circle is beginning to formulate, this is the command center where we can meet and promote each other's work, as well as our own. Look up Steve School and send a friend request, feel free to post your books on my pages, to do this simply go to amazon and find your book, while you are there click the pinterest, twitter and face book icons and share your book to those sites, then in front of those icons you will see the word share, click on that and the amazon link for your book will appear, copy this link and return to face book, you can post on this on all of my pages, I now have close to two dozen face book pages and growing.

Some of my pages are dedicated specifically to the subject of book promotion. On these pages simply post your books, like the page, invite your friends to like the page, and then share the page. Now look at all the other books on the page, to be successful in marketing our books into the big numbers, it requires a system of links and reviews to be built, the links increase our visibility and the reviews increase our sales. This is why I am building a network of motivated authors which I call my winners circle, you are welcome to climb aboard if you are motivated, and have integrity. We do not need flakes or slow pokes to hold us back, we need hard chargers in the winner's circle.

The basic plan is that we meet on my promotional pages, we review each other's books at sites like Amazon and Barnes and Noble, this is called an author review swap, the more good reviews that you have the more sales you will get, the basic guide line is that you need to have at least thirty positive reviews with an average rating of 3.5 stars or better per book. Do you want to wait ten years for this to happen or do you want it now?, before the subject matter of your book becomes obsolete or the dollar crashes and the economy gets worse? Motivated hard chargers get results. We can simply purchase each other's books, read them, and review them online, then use the amazon social media icons to share each others work (as well as our own) with the rest of the world.

I would like for my winners circle to be a well oiled machine, so that when we fire up this machine we get big results right now, not next week or next month or next year. It only takes a few minutes to knock out these small tasks that I have outlined here, I receive an email notification that you have reviewed my book if the review is done on amazon, once I find this email and am at a suitable internet connection, it will only take me about five minutes to share, tweet, review, and pin your book. This also means that if you want to wait two weeks to review my book, then it will be two weeks before I find the review and return the favor. Do you want to wait two weeks to get your five star review, or do you want to simply fire up the machine and get results right now? Two week increments add up and multiply into years, I would like to get one million sales right now, this month, not gradually build up to it over the next ten years, so get motivated, get on my community pages, and get active. We can greatly expedite the process of swapping author reviews by simply purchasing each other's books in electronic E book format, so that we can download and read much faster than waiting for the printed book to come in the mail.

The more products that you publish the better, I already have more than twenty, I will add more every year, so there is plenty of tweeting and review swapping to do. Notice that my books are on a wide variety of subjects, the more variety of subjects that you pin and tweet about, the more variety of followers that you attract and the larger your customer base becomes. These followers are our bread and butter, they buy, share and re tweet our products across the globe, causing our publicity to go viral. At the end of this book you will see a list of titles that I have published. Since this book is available in E book format the search engines can see those titles and this helps to increase my visibility in search results, it also tends to link my books together, so that you might search for one of my titles and pull up several of them, you might be researching a particular subject online and pull up a whole bunch of my books even if you were not looking for them, and that is my goal, to get my products in front of as many people as possible.
The next time that you watch a you tube video, click the share icon underneath the video, you will see several icons appear for various social media site, all of those can be used to promote your products all over the world.

There are more social media sites that we need to use to promote out work, I will cover more of this now, some of them are very basic and will not require much explanation, you can simply book mark the sites, register, fill out a profile, post pictures of your books as well as links to your sales pages and after this there is simply the basics of inviting friends, sending friend requests, and sharing, commenting and liking things. Here is a basic list of these extra sites.

Myspace.
Linkdin.
Flicker.

Flickr is one of my favorite sites, here you can upload pictures and videos. You can also post links in the comment section for each post, and you can attach tons of keywords, and keyword phrases to your uploads. I have uploaded my books and promotional videos all over this site. I will post the same book cover picture multiple time with each one having different keywords attached to it to hopefully increase my appearance in the search results.

I now have over forty promotional videos on youtube and I will be creating two more of them today, I like to create at least one or more videos for each book that I publish. I also like to create a face book community page for each book that I publish and it only takes me a few minutes to do the basic page set up, once it is there it can be found in search results and begin to get likes on its own, as well as by being promoted. Make sure that on your promotional pages all of your privacy settings are set to public, otherwise the internet search engines will not be able to share your page with the world.

I was able to create my own website, it was very fast, simple and easy to do as well as inexpensive. I was able to post my book covers, key words, and links to my sales pages, as well as two of my youtube videos. You might be better than me at creating your website, but I feel that mine serves my purpose, it was created at Yola.

Here is a tidbit of information that you might find useful if you are good with computers, this advice was shared with me from a professional marketing director from a large and very successful company.

If you are creating a website, sometimes you can change the back ground color, and sometimes you can change the font color as well, the important secret here is that whether this digital product is a web site, web page, or electronic book, the search engines can see inside of this product. Therefore if I have a white back ground, and type key words and key word phrases onto this white page, using white font, you will not be able to see those key words, but the search engines will, they will see these keywords and consider them when placing this product into the search results which I can use to my advantage. What if I was to write Joe's pizzeria here in white font, would people searching for Joe's pizzeria find this E book in their search results?,   possibly. They might not be looking for this book, they might not even be interested in it, but my goal is to get my product in front of them anyway just in case they might buy it, and by doing so I have planted a seed which will grow and multiply, if I do not promote my work, I simply publish it and let nature take its course, how many people will see my book per day? Three?, ten?, fifteen? Of those few persons who manage to somehow find my book buried deeply in the search results by accident or some sort of stroke of pure luck, how many of them do you suppose will actually buy my product, one percent?, three percent?, what if I promoted my work, on my own, by myself, with no help from anyone, how many potential customers could I bring to my work now?

The answer is that with some effort I probably could get hundreds of people per day to see my books, if I am intelligent I can get thousands of people to see my products every day all over the world, if I am both intelligent and highly motivated (which I am), I can get hundreds of thousands of people per day to see the items that I have for sale, I could even potentially get millions of persons to see this book. The more people who see this book, the more sales that I will get for this book, and the more potential customers that I will be literally dragging to my other products.

Now imagine if you will, having a winner's circle, of intelligent, motivated authors, networking together to promote each other's work, moving swiftly like a well oiled machine, what kind of promotional power do we wield directly at our finger tips?, what can we accomplish with this ultra powerful tool?, the answer is quite simple, when we fire up this book promoting machine, at the push of a button, at the click of an icon, at the scroll of the mouse, we can instantly place our work in front of hundreds of millions of people.

Let us say that two persons out of a hundred, will actually buy my book, this is a fair number to assume, it might be more but probably not less, 2 percent is an easily attainable goal, now by simply publishing my book and doing a small (tiny) amount of promotion, two hundred people see my work today, this nets me a total of four sales. At 99 cents per E book I will average about $1.60 commission depending on which sites that it sold from, even with the possible variables this number is very close.

Now let us say that we formed our winners circle, brought it up to speed with about three dozen highly motivated authors all working together, suddenly the machine is fired up, at the push of the button, this book was just placed in front of 240 million people online, literally set in front of them on their computer screen. At a sales rate of two percent average buy ratio, what kind of money has this little 99 cent E book just made for me?

I could break out the calculator and come up with a logical number, or I could just simply say, I don't know, but it sounds like a lot!

Either way, I will be relaxing by the pool, and soaking up some sun this summer, which sounds better to me than having to go to work every day.

It is my birthday, and it is the first day of the rest of my life, there is a thick, juicy, steak waiting for me with my name on it, this steak is cooked to perfection, and it is calling my name, the question that I pose to you is,

Will I see you in the winner's circle?

Happy new year,
Steven School. 12-31-2013

The first DVD that I published which was in 2013, is called The Magnum Opus

www.createspace.com/381734

The second DVD that I am publishing now is called Alchemy and the Athanor, journey into the fire.

www.createspace.com/388897

I am publishing more instructional DVD's on a wide variety of subjects.

Alchemy books that I have published.
Alchemy and the green lion
Alchemy and the golden water
Alchemy and the peacocks tail
Alchemy and the golden process
Alchemy and the ravens head
Alchemy and the tincture of gold
Sol and Luna the hermetical wedding
Alchemy survival guide
Aurum Solis, Gold of the Sun

ABOUT THE AUTHOR

I enjoy cooking at home from scratch, I like writing and have been interested in becoming an author for many years. Thanks to Amazon my dream has become a reality. I enjoy the company of my Rottweilers, I also enjoy the hermetic arts and have been studying Alchemy diligently since 2008 with an emphasis on the white and red philosophers stones, the Elixir of life, and the primum ens mellissa.
I was born in the winter.

Other books that I have written.
Casino survival guide, breaking the bank
Chinese takeout recipes
The Kitchen Ninja
The Kitchen ninja 2
Grandmas delicious recipes
Trophy wife
How to make money
Booze survival guide
Wilderness survival tips
Karate secrets revealed, knowledge of the masters
Kitchen survival guide
The secret recipe book, kitchen tool box

This book will be available as a printed book, as well as a digital E book because this will allow me to reach a much broader audience.

One last bit of advice, look up any video on you tube, click the share icon underneath the video, you will see about a dozen social media sites pop up, all free tools for you to promote your work.

facebook.com/steve.school.

STEVEN SCHOOL

http://www.howtomakethephilosophersstone.com